MW01629249
A
LITTLE
BIRD
told me
VOLUME 1
melody ross
XOXO
melody ross

Published by Brave Girls Club, Inc., September 2012
1309 N 39th Street, Suite 110, Nampa, ID 83687

ISBN 978-0-9846660-0-3

Written and illustrated by Melody Ross
Edited and compiled by Kathy Wilkins

contents

Dear Beautiful, Phenomenal You,

There was a time in my life when I was very very very broken...
a time when I truly believed that I would always be broken.
So many lies ran through my head and my heart,
breaking me even more.

One day I closed my eyes and asked....
"What is the truth about who I am?"
and
"What is the truth about the painful life situations I keep
finding myself in...what do they mean about me?"

Inside of this book are the answers I received as I spent many
days in solitude asking those questions over and over again.

I wrote these messages down because I knew they were not
just for me...but for every single girl alive.

These are messages from "a little bird" .... an all-loving little
bird who really knows a thing or two about the truth...and about you,
and about me.

My biggest hope is that you will really let yourself believe all
of these words in this book...because I know that they are true about
you...I know it without a single doubt.

You are so very very very loved.
xoxo

melody ross

This book
is dedicated
to the source of all
sweet, healing,
beautiful truth.
The loving truth that is
for all of us.

Invite
HAPPY
whenever possible

Dear Joyful Girl,

One of the best ways to nourish your soul is to seek out and do things that totally absorb you in happiness, things that call to you, things that you are naturally good at, and things that fill you up.

It is important to balance the things that MUST be done with the things that we do simply because of the JOY that comes from doing them.

Life is meant to be enjoyed and not merely endured.

There are simple and small things that we can do to refuel our souls....

We all need to make time to do these things if we want to live meaningful lives. We will be better at everything we MUST do if we take time to do what we LOVE to do. We will be better wives, mothers, friends, daughters, sisters, aunts, partners, and coworkers....and we surely will FEEL better and more joyful every minute of the day.

Please don't get sucked into the falsehood that taking time to nourish your soul is selfish and futile. It is ESSENTIAL. It doesn't take anything away from anyone... it only adds to the goodness that you already have inside of you.

Be brave today and do something that puts a smile on your face...simply for the sake of doing it. Little miracles will begin to happen...you'll see.

You are so very loved. xoxo

ENJOY Life

just
keep being
your
beautiful
wild
funky
self.

Dear Beloved Girl,

From the prints of the tips of your fingers and toes...to the way the flecks in your eyes catch the light in ways that have never happened in all of history, to the shape of your nose combined with the shape of your ears...to the way your laughter carries through the air in waves that are unique to you...you are a marvel.

You are a perfectly, carefully created marvel.

There may be days when you feel that you don't measure up, that your life is of no consequence and may not matter as much as someone else's life. There may be days when you feel invisible, irrelevent, and simply one of billions.

You are not simply one of billions.
YOU ARE ONE IN BILLIONS.

Of the billions of human beings alive at this moment, there is not another one exactly like you. There is not another who has the exact ideas that you have. There is not one who has the same heart desires that you have. There is not one who has had the same experiences that you have had.

NEVER minimize the value of YOU. If our Creator was not so particular about each masterpiece, each of us would look the same, sound the same, do the same. We are each a unique contributor. We each make a difference. We each matter...so much.

Please don't ever forget this important truth.
You are valuable.

And you are so loved.
xoxo

FORGIVE
YOUR
SELF

Dear Merciful Girl,

What if...WHAT IF...today was the day that you chose to stop blaming yourself for choices you have made...choices you would make differently today, knowing what you know now and being who you are now. What if today you put your arm around yourself, kissed yourself smack on the cheeck and said,

"I know better now, so I can do better now."

...and then let it be done, once and for all.
No more blame, no more shame.

Then...what if that made you feel loved and safe enough to take all of the responsibility for those choices and turn those choices into fuel to feed your beautiful new life with wisdom and experience?

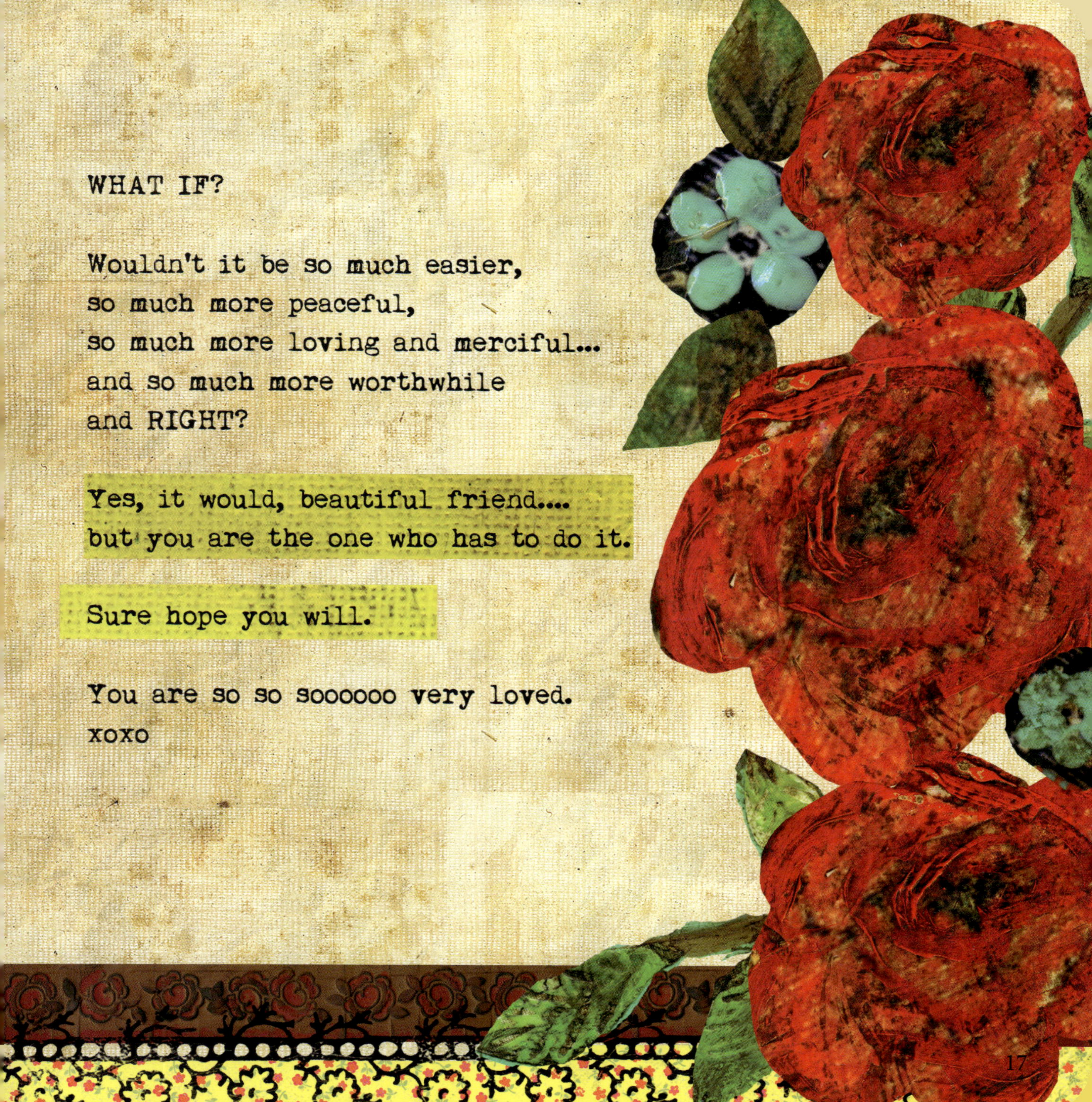

WHAT IF?

Wouldn't it be so much easier,
so much more peaceful,
so much more loving and merciful...
and so much more worthwhile
and RIGHT?

Yes, it would, beautiful friend....
but you are the one who has to do it.

Sure hope you will.

You are so so soooooo very loved.
xoxo

FLY
AWAY

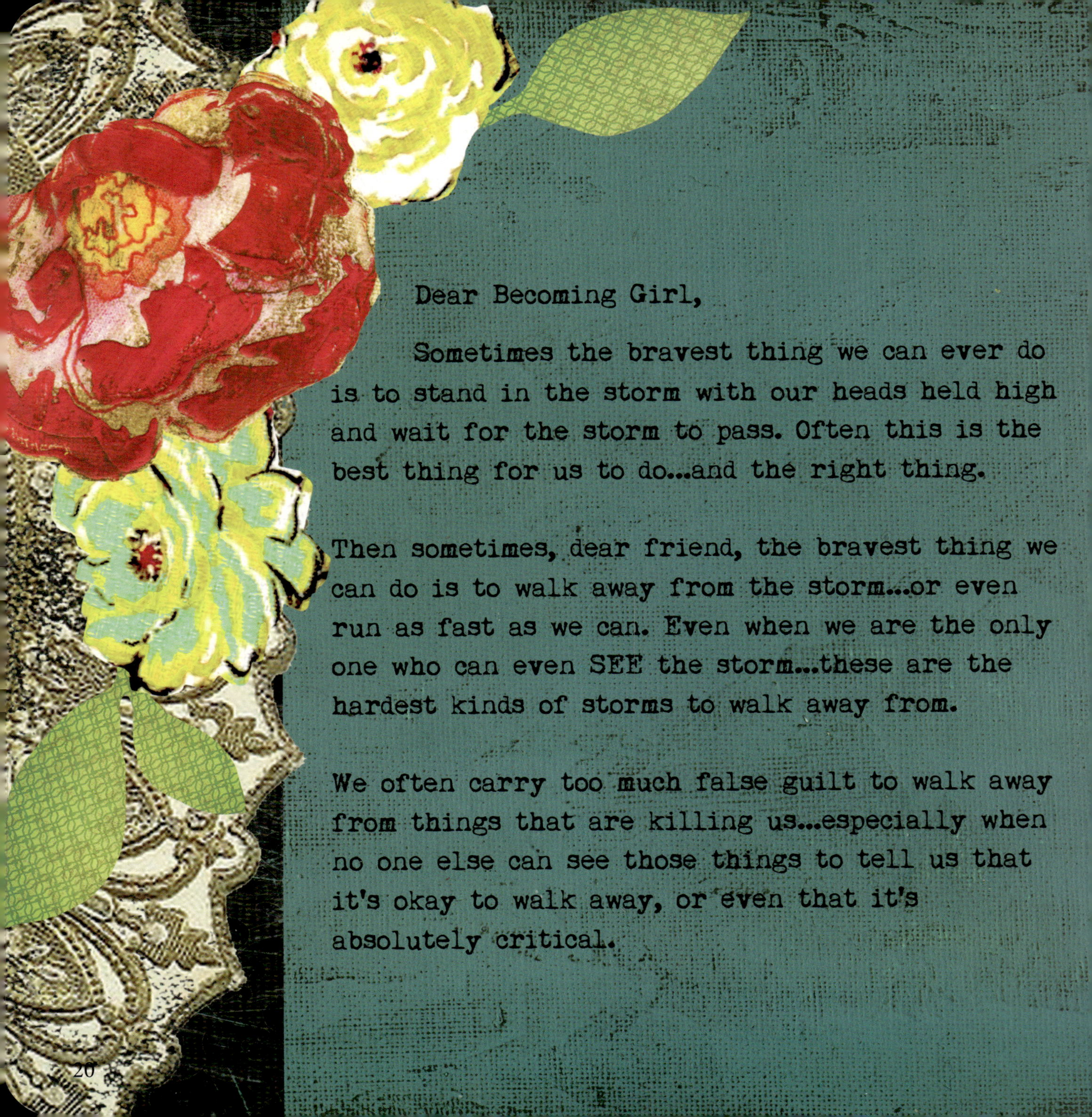

Dear Becoming Girl,

Sometimes the bravest thing we can ever do is to stand in the storm with our heads held high and wait for the storm to pass. Often this is the best thing for us to do...and the right thing.

Then sometimes, dear friend, the bravest thing we can do is to walk away from the storm...or even run as fast as we can. Even when we are the only one who can even SEE the storm...these are the hardest kinds of storms to walk away from.

We often carry too much false guilt to walk away from things that are killing us...especially when no one else can see those things to tell us that it's okay to walk away, or even that it's absolutely critical.

Sometimes our deepest agony is caused by things so private that no one else can see. Sometimes we are hurt by things that are so secret, so private, that it is hard to see how devastating they are to us because there is no light shed on them. In the darkness, lies are whispered to us...telling us that we deserve abuse, or that we brought it on ourselves.

Your soul knows, sweetheart.

In the deepest parts of yourself, your soul knows the truth. Your soul longs for light...not darkness. Your soul longs to be cared for, not abused. To walk away from any kind of abuse is brave, powerful, and critical to the life of your soul.

You can do it, beautiful soul...and you must. NO ONE deserves to be abused, and NO ONE has the right to abuse you.

You are loved. And you deserve to be loved.
xoxo

say
it

Dear Kind-Hearted Girl,

If there's a conversation in your life that needs to take place, maybe now is the time to do it.

If there's someone you need to make amends with, someone you need to express gratitude to, someone you need to tell how much they mean to you...it's a great time to do it. If your heart is pushing you to do it, you won't feel at peace until you do.

You never know when you have the elixer to heal someone else's pain. Your words could be the very words that someone needs to be able to move forward.

Hearing the words come out of your own mouth might just change your own life, too. Sometimes the words we need to say heal our own pain.

Whether you write it or say it...have the conversation. You will be amazed at what transpires when you have the difficult conversation that you need to have.

Relationships are important. YOU are important. And if you are carrying around the weight of words that need to be spoken, just do it. Even if it seems scary.

You can do it. You are a brave, brave girl, and you are so very loved.
xoxo

SEE
SOULS

Dear Insightful Girl,

Miraculous things happen when people know that you believe in them. Beautiful, miraculous things happen when YOU know that others believe in YOU.

This knowledge brings with it some important responsibilities.

First, it is so important that others know of our faith in them, of the way that we see them and their potential.

Second, it is SO VERY CRITICAL that we spend our time with others who believe in US.

Not many things are more exhilarating than being around people who SEE who we really are, and then go out of their way to TELL us the very truth about what they see.

Seek out these people...you deserve it and you need it.

At the same time, go out and BE that person to others, to as many others as you can. We can change the world in little ways... little ways that are very very big.

Choose to stay where the beautiful in life is. You are loved.
xoxo

You have permission

Dear Amazing Girl,

Why is it that so many of us don't feel we have a right to do the things we want to do, to dream big dreams, or to be who we want to be?

Why do we think there are special hoops we have to jump through, or people we have to ask first, or stuff we have to do first?

Well, amazing friend...no more excuses.

Here is your Official Permission Slip...

Dear World,

This fabulous brave girl has permission to go out and be amazing, to have all the happiness in the world, and to make a difference in ways that only she can. I know, world, that you do not require permission, but for some reason, this lovely girl keeps thinking she needs it. So please keep supporting her, keep teaching her, and keep showing her exactly how amazing she really is.

Sincerely,
Her Biggest Fan

Now...GET OUT THERE AND DO IT!!! You are gonna knock everyone's socks off!!

You are so loved.
XOXO

Be
in
charge

Dear Had-Enough Girl,

First, take a second and breathe, okay?...deep, deep, deeply breathe in and out...Close your eyes for a minute and remember that it's okay if you feel completely overwhelmed at the tasks that are ahead for you, at the choices you have to make, and at the burden of responsibility you are feeling. It's tough to be a grown up, isn't it?

It's okay if you just want to throw a fit some days and let someone else be in charge.

Now that you have that out of your system, think for a minute about how you want the rest of the day (and tomorrow) to go...how you really want to feel, what you really want to accomplish, where you really want to end up.

Decide right this second that you are going to DO ONE THING to take a step in that direction. When that thing is done, do another.

Don't let yucky feelings be in charge. YOU are in charge of how the rest of your day goes inside of your skin, head, and heart. YOU ARE STRONG ENOUGH to choose how you REALLY want to feel. You really are. No matter what just happened, no matter what you fear about what might happen next. You get to be in charge of how it goes for YOU right now.

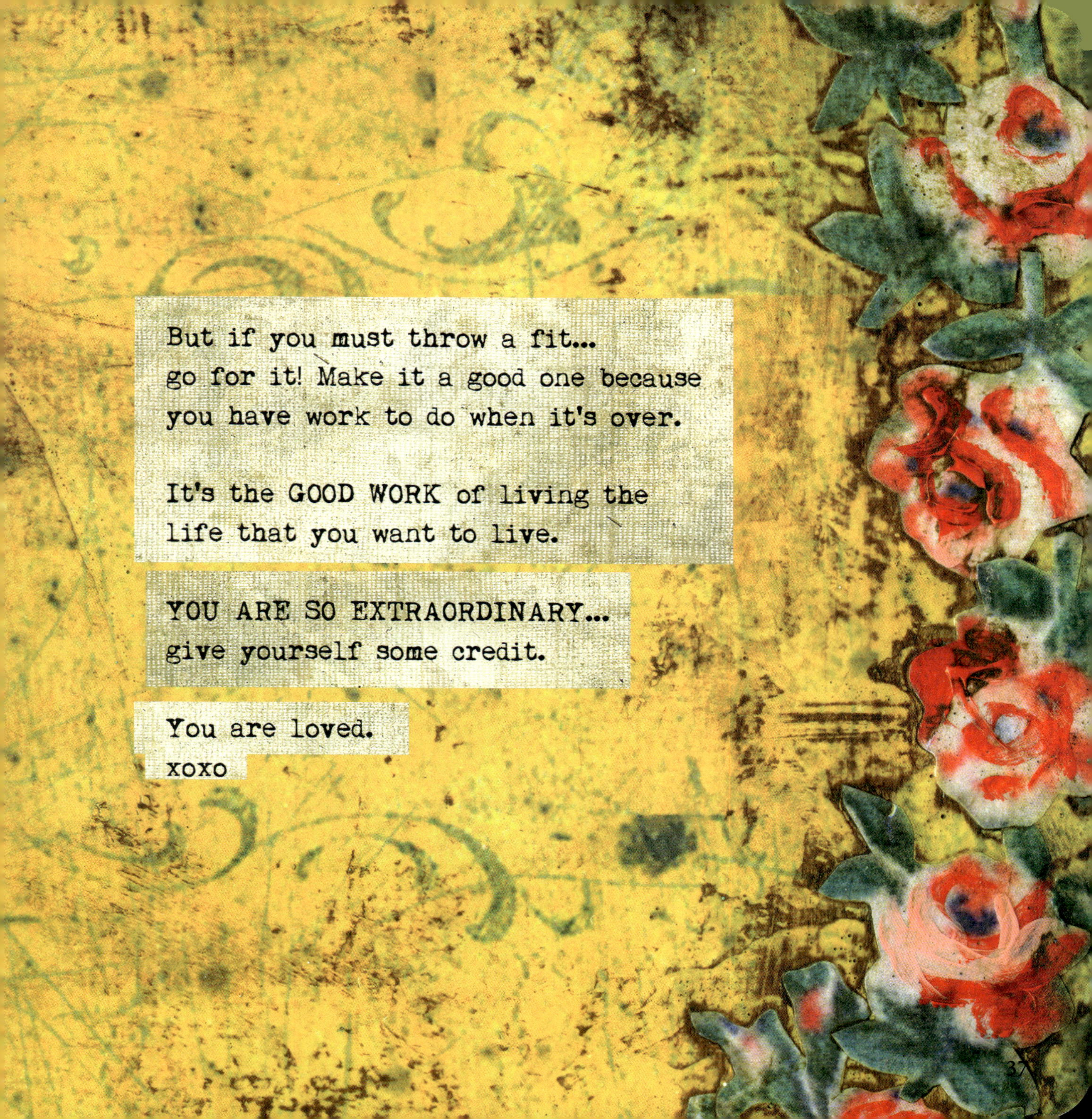

But if you must throw a fit...
go for it! Make it a good one because
you have work to do when it's over.

It's the GOOD WORK of living the
life that you want to live.

YOU ARE SO EXTRAORDINARY...
give yourself some credit.

You are loved.
xoxo

CHOOSE LIGHT

Dear Brave Girl,

Think for a bit about the nature of light. Light is something very special. Now think about the nature of darkness. Sometimes we are tricked into believing that light and darkness are equal. But they are not, and there is such a lesson there.

Light is energy and truth and beauty and illumination and brilliance...love.

Darkness is simply a lack of light. It is nothing else.

There are things in life that try to trick us the same way, somehow making us believe that they are bigger and scarier than they are. Fears are this way. Lies are this way. Fears and lies LOVE to grow in the dark.

Light always wins. A tiny light can put out the biggest dark...but dark never has the power to put out light.

Truth always wins. Love always wins.

So, when there is a choice to be made, bring it into the light. Stay in the light and step out of the darkness when you find you have been pulled in that direction.

Choose truth. Choose love. Always always always go where the peace is. Always choose the light.

You are so very loved.

xoxo

OH
HAPPY
DAY

Dear Brilliant Girl,

Sometimes when we get really really really honest with ourselves, we realize we have been putting everything aside while we wait for something big to happen.

We decide that we'll bring the beautiful and soul-deep things we want to do and be back out into the daylight once that 'big thing' standing in the way has happened.

It's time to stop waiting.

It's time to become who you want to become and do what you want to do and learn what you want to learn and rest when you want to rest..to take little pieces of time and do terrific things with them that are beautiful and personal and unique and true.

If we are truly honest, we have no idea how long that wait will be, and it is not worth it to lose minutes, days, weeks, months, and years of our lives waiting around for something that might never happen the way we think it's going to happen.

Every day we can make progress toward our own big and little dreams. No more waiting, okay?

It is time. It's time to find peace...time to be happy... time to really live. It is time. Today.

You are so loved.
xoxo

you are enough

Dear More-Than-Enough Girl,

One of the most painful traps we can ever fall into is the ENOUGH trap.

This is the trap with an ugly cycle that tells us that no matter how much we do, how hard we work, how much we have, how much we try...it is NEVER ENOUGH.

If you've had a day when you've done all you can and you still feel defeated, please dear one, give yourself some grace.

You are the only one who can decide that it is enough, that you have done enough, that you have enough, and especially that you ARE enough. These are truths that you must accept for yourself... no one else can do this for you.

When the day is done, be kind enough to let yourself be done with the day, with the satisfaction of knowing that you have done all you could do...and that it was enough.

Lay your head down and know that tomorrow is a BRAND NEW DAY, that you don't have to pack every expectation or worry with you from the day before, the month before, the year before...but that you get to pack light and let it be a brand new day.

You are enough. You've done enough.
You have enough. You are brave enough.

You are absolutely loved enough, too.
xoxo

Life
wants
to
LOVE
you

Dear Uncommon Girl,

We live in a world that goes sooooo fast..faster and faster every day it seems. We are bombarded with information, theories, philosophies, stories, photos, ideas, inspiration, CONSTANTLY.

It's hard to feel like it's okay to STOP and just be. It's hard to feel like it's okay to be in our skin JUST THE WAY IT IS. It's hard to feel like it's okay to feel like we are OKAY RIGHT NOW. There is always something faster, better, shinier, fancier, cooler, more innovative, ground-breaking, earth-shattering, life-changing that we are told we MUST HAVE or MUST DO so that we can FINALLY BE OKAY.

You are okay right now.

Don't let this fast-paced world convince you that you must keep striving, seeking, changing, polishing, upgrading, overloading...

...trading in, trading up, keeping up...WHEW... just to START to feel okay with who you are.

Sit and listen to your breath. When it tells you that you are okay, that you are just right, THAT is the truth.

Every day there are things we can work on doing better. There are things we can learn. There are ways we can grow. This is true! But right now...YOU, exactly as you are, you are okay right now. It is okay to be happy. It is okay to feel at peace. It is okay to be content. It is okay to crave simplicity.

Listen to your heart. Go where the peace is.

LOVE LIFE. LOVE YOURSELF. LOVE OTHERS. Do your best and then let yourself be.

Right now, today...you are so very loved.
xoxo

DO
CRAZY
GOOD
THINGS

Dear Sparkling Girl,

Sometimes the craziest things can pop into our heads.

Sometimes little urges just keep poking at us, prodding us, elbowing us. They won't give up. We KNOW we should say something, or do something, or write something, or show up somewhere, or give something away, or call someone, or make the first move with an idea....

BUT IT IS JUST TOO SCARY.

SOUL DEEP urges are little sparkles of magic that are seeds to VERY BIG THINGS.

Sometimes we are the ONLY ONE who has the seed, and if we don't plant it, the big amazing thing will never grow.

Sometimes we have JUST THE RIGHT MEDICINE for someone else's soul sickness. Sometimes we have the very idea that will change EVERYTHING. Sometimes we are the answer to someone's desperate prayers.

So, dear girl...even if it's scary, scarier than you could ever even express...

DO IT ANYWAY. Very important things depend on it. It is no coincidence. It is the real deal.

You are so very loved, so very needed...and that voice in your heart is WISER THAN WISE. Trust it.

xoxo

BE NOT AFRAID

Dear Lovely Girl,

We often forget an essential part of what it means to renew, restore, recharge, or start over.

We have to let go of our old skin, our old baggage, our old ways of thinking, our old beliefs about who we are.

Even when we are doing our best to hang on to new truths... new experiences..new ways of being that are right and good, we can still be weighed down by things we have not let go.

If our new life continues to be weighed down by our old life, our old skin...by old destructive relationships or habits or behaviors, it holds us back, slows us down, and makes us constantly doubt ourselves and our brand new skin.

Don't ever feel bad about shedding old outdated weight that has no soulful usefulness in your life anymore. This can come in so many forms...and all of them make us feel heavy with burden.

Think of a butterfly carrying its cocoon around for the rest of its flying life, just because it was part of its past...part of its journey to becoming a butterfly.

It is okay to leave the past behind. You won't fly the way you were meant to fly or to the heights you are meant to reach until you do.

You are so very very loved. It's time to let it go and embrace the NOW.

You are so spectacular
under all that stuff!

xoxo

let it go

Dear Gutsy Girl,

Don't be afraid to face your giants. Don't be afraid to stand face to face and toe to toe with what scares you the most. Don't be afraid to pull the things that taunt you out from the darkness into the light so you can see them clearly.

Our fears, our hurts, and our biggest hold-backs often lose all their power once they are brought into the light to be seen for what they truly are.. Many time they are figurative bullies...not much more. Many times our fears have no merit, our hurts are not worth the energy we put into them, and the things holding us back are things we have outgrown long ago.

We hold onto things for years, letting them linger and grow in the background, in the closets, deep in our hearts, when all we need to do is pull them out and see if they really should hold ANY more of our energy or our brain space.

It doesn't make us weak to let go of old garbage. It doesn't make us weak to forgive and move on. It is a sign of strength and character...a way to take control of our own futures, our own feelings, our own place in the world.

It's so much sunnier, warmer, prettier and happier in the light.

Shine on, lovely friend. You are loved.
xoxo

YOU ARE
DOING
JUST FINE

Dear Incomparable girl,
Comparing is a yucky habit that never has a happy ending. Life hands each of us different 'kits' full of different stuff, and comparing one set of skills, circumstances, attributes, looks, or relationships to another is like comparing water to fire and wanting them to be exactly the same...even though we need both water and fire almost every day of our lives.
If you are feeling discontented, try to see if it's because you are comparing.

Take comparing completely out of the equation and see how you feel now...See??

When you take out all of the comparing, you see that you actually have exactly what YOU need right now, and that you are doing just fine.

Comparing takes away our joy and our gratitude and our authenticity. Instead of comparing, practice feeling happy about another's abundance. And feel grateful and happy about YOURS, too.

See your life for what it is. See YOUR gifts, YOUR path, and YOUR mission. That's where your influence is. That's where all the magic in your life will happen. That's where you will find the most JOY. Isn't that where you want to be?

Of course it is! xoxo

you are absolutely spectacular

LIVE BIG
you
don't
have
to
stay
stuck

Dear Precious Girl,

You don't always have to be so tough, you know. There are people who want to help and would jump at the chance if they knew what you really need and want. There are so many people who love you. You don't have to carry your burdens alone.

Have you ever isolated yourself, stuck in survival mode, forgetting that there is anything else to think about beyond how to get through the next day? or even the next few minutes?

Life is not meant for that kind of living. The good news is that there are things you can do right now to get your beautiful self out of that kind of stuck-ness.

Today is a good day to reach out. Call a friend and be really honest about where you are.

Try something new...a new skill, a new recipe, a new route to the same old places. This will help you get unstuck and begin to build a life that is about THRIVING and ENJOYING rather than surviving and enduring.

You are so strong and so great at surviving and enduring, friend. But everyone who loves you wants more for you than that. YOUR SOUL wants more than that, too...you know that, right?

You can do this. There are so many smiles and laughs and friendships and adventures ahead for you. Your best years have not even been lived yet! You have so much to look forward to. Decide to LIVE BIG!!!

xoxo

Choose to
forgive

Dear Cherished Girl,

What is it about forgiveness that is so difficult, even when holding a grudge, holding on to hurt, or holding on to painful memories makes us feel so rotten?

Forgiving someone doesn't mean allowing them into your life. It doesn't mean that you are saying that an injustice hasn't been done, or that you are okay with what happened.

Forgiveness is a magic little decision you make to free YOURSELF.

Bad feelings, horrid memories and grudges are little daggers that carve away at your soul. Those daggers come with handcuffs and chains. Who wants to live like that? Who CAN live like that without it completely holding us back from the lovely life that was meant for us?

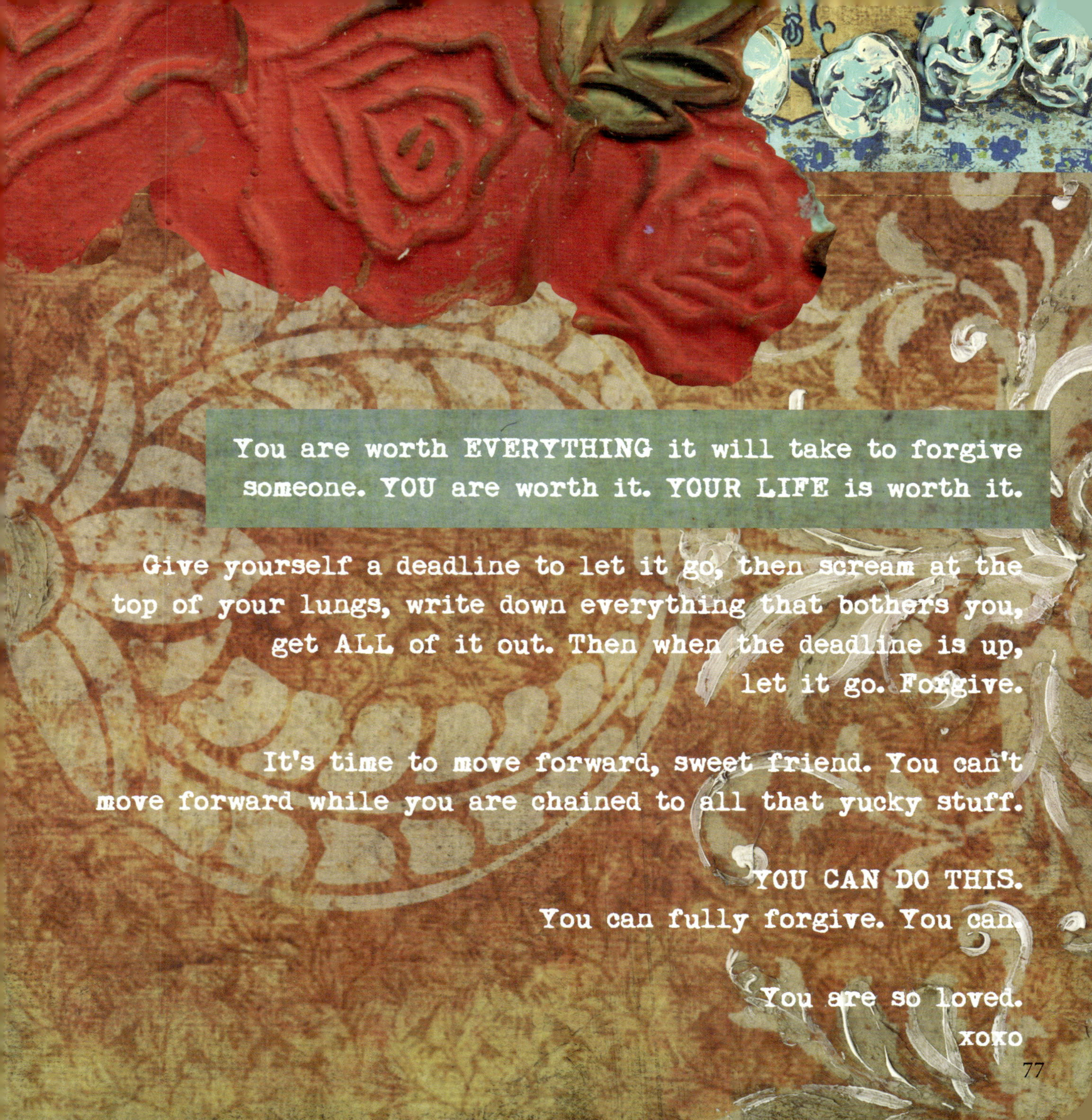

You are worth EVERYTHING it will take to forgive someone. YOU are worth it. YOUR LIFE is worth it.

Give yourself a deadline to let it go, then scream at the top of your lungs, write down everything that bothers you, get ALL of it out. Then when the deadline is up, let it go. Forgive.

It's time to move forward, sweet friend. You can't move forward while you are chained to all that yucky stuff.

YOU CAN DO THIS.
You can fully forgive. You can.

You are so loved.
xoxo

rest
BRAVE

Dear Wild & Free Girl,

You are doing so many good things. You are going so many wonderful directions. You are spreading so much goodness and kindness and wild-happy energy.

You are making goals and dreaming dreams and trying to do even better than you did yesterday.

You are thinking about people you love and how you can serve them. You are a loyal friend and family member. You are making an enormous difference in the lives of all who know you and in so many lives you dont even know about, too.

PLEASE REST

It is time to give yourself a break & to stop and thank your body and your soul for everything it does to keep you going. This would be a great time to pat yourself on the back and take a nap or a hot bath...even eat some chocolate! Sure, there are still lots of things for you to work on...

and you will get to that. You are doing great, and sometimes you just have to stop and let yourself breathe, evaluate...rest...recharge...restore. Take good care of yourself, fabulous friend! We need all the fabulousness of you!

You are so very loved.

xoxo

KEEP GOING

Dear Persevering Girl,

Think of a time when you almost gave up,
almost quit, almost threw in the towel.
But you decided to give it one more shot.

Where did that decision take you? Maybe you had to decide over and over again not to quit at something. Maybe now it has developed into something so wonderful that you can't imagine being fully alive without that as part of your life.

Maybe it's a skill you've developed.
Maybe it's your marriage, or a friendship, or a fitness program or the business that had a slow and scary start.

Just think back on
all the times you wanted to quit
but you didn't.

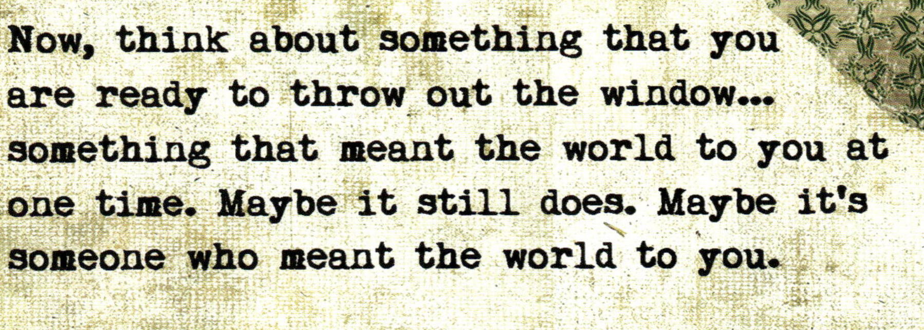

Now, think about something that you are ready to throw out the window... something that meant the world to you at one time. Maybe it still does. Maybe it's someone who meant the world to you.

Maybe, just maybe, it would be totally worth it to give it one more shot, to keep going. What do you have to lose?

So often in life, it's that last mile in the marathon that shows us what it's all about. Don't quit before the race is over.

You are so loved.
xoxo

you will fly again

Dear Deserving Girl,
You were born to fly.
You were born to spread your wings.
You were born with the ability
and the right to make choices for your life.
You were not born a bird to be caged.

Here is the definition of freedom:

free-dom (noun)

1. The quality or state of being free as, a: the absence of necessity, coercion, or constraint in choice or action, b: liberation from slavery or restraint or from the power of another, c: the quality or state of being exempt or released from something onerous.

If there is ANYTHING in your life that makes you feel like you are in captivity, confined, imprisoned, limited, in slavery, restrained, or restricted at a soul level... please please please, beautiful girl, listen to your soul.

So many souls suffer in silent captivity. Please do whatever it takes to help your soul to be free.

You are beloved. xoxo

rough days
HAPPEN

Dear Authentic Girl,

If emotional funks didn't show up in our lives from time to time, we probably wouldn't stop and look at what we are doing, how we are doing it, and what the consequences are of being off track.

Funks kind of stop us in our tracks. Even though they feel uncomfortable and sometimes scary, they stop us and make us think. They also make us appreciate happiness so much more once the funk is over.

Don't be afraid of funks. Sure, they are highly annoying. They show up when you don't really have the time or energy to deal with them, and they sometimes stay longer than they could possibly be needed. But they sure do make us want to change some things when they come...

...so, because of this they are really a gift. They are one of those paradoxical gifts of opposition that taste bitter and therefore make us appreciate the sweet parts of our lives.

Those gifts whip us into action and make us stop settling for things that we should not be settling for. They get us back on track so many times. They show us where to turn for comfort and who our friends are.

Roll with it, baby. The funk will be over before you know it. It will be gone as fast as it came, and it will leave lots of gifts if you are open to receiving them.

You are just right. You will be smiling and dancing again soon!

You are so very loved.
xoxo

be
kind

Dear Spectacular Girl,

The world shows us a brand of 'normal' that is pretty much unachievable. Sweet friend, be careful what you allow in your life from the media and from what is sold to us as what the ideal life, the ideal body, and the ideal relationship should look like.

Models are photo-shopped and social lives are exaggerated and extravagant lifestyles are made 'normal'. It is easy to get sucked into a place where we believe that this is reality for everyone but us. This leaves us feeling profoundly lonely or wrong...feeling like we have to compromise what we believe in our hearts just so we can fit in.

Just get quiet, lovely. Ask yourself what is beautiful and true.

Ask yourself what matters to YOU.

Ask yourself what is of lasting value...what will bring the most joy and peace into your life.

Then...be brave enough to go after THOSE answers even if they are the opposite of what 'they' say is right.

Your instincts are right. Your heart is good. You really do know the answers. You are not the only one who feels the way you feel. You are brave, strong, and beautiful, and you get to choose the kind of life you want to have, even if it isn't in a magazine.

Be kind to yourself.
You are so deeply loved.
xoxo

it is going to be ok

Dear Treasured Girl,

When things we cherish are stripped from our lives, it can feel like we can't live life with the same intensity or passion or joy ever again.

This is just not true, lovely girl.

Even if we've lost all of our money, we can still have grand and beautiful adventures. We can make anything an adventure...in fact, learning to live without money can be one of the most wonderful adventures there is!

If we lose people that we love, we truly can still love and be loved. We can cherish wonderful memories and let painful ones go. More wonderful people will show up in our lives as soon as we are ready.

Even when a career change is required and it feels scary and devastating, this can be the beginning of something new that we never would have experienced otherwise.

Making the most of where we are is how we live with intensity, passion and joy. Making do with what we have spurs creativity and resourcefulness that would not have been necessary otherwise.

Reframe it, dear friend. See the possibilities even when it feels like you've just had the wind knocked out of you.

Your life is meant to be filled with passion and joy. If you can't find it, make it! We can create happiness and beauty out of whatever we have (or don't have) right now.

You are so loved...never forgotten...
always always always loved.
xoxo

She did it
ANYWAY

Dear Fabulous Girl,

You may feel too old or maybe too young. You may feel too fat or too uneducated or too worn out or too wounded or too broken.

You might sometimes even feel that it's just not worth it to try so hard, or that your clothes aren't just right, or that your car is too embarrassing.

You may feel like you are too unorganized, inefficient or inexperienced to start on your dreams or to keep going on your dreams.

You may feel like the world is too unkind or that it is all just too scary. You might even feel like your dreams are sort of silly...or that they don't matter.

Yes, you might feel this way. There may be others who cause you to feel this way. You probably have a hundred good excuses not to follow your dreams, not to live the life you want to live, not to WAKE UP and FLY...reasons to stay stuck.

Your excuses might even be really legitimate.

Well, dear friend...DO IT ANYWAY. DREAM ANYWAY. FLY ANYWAY!! Okay? No more waiting.
DO IT ANYWAY.

You are so capable. You are so loved. It is TIME.
xoxo

it will
get better
(it really will)

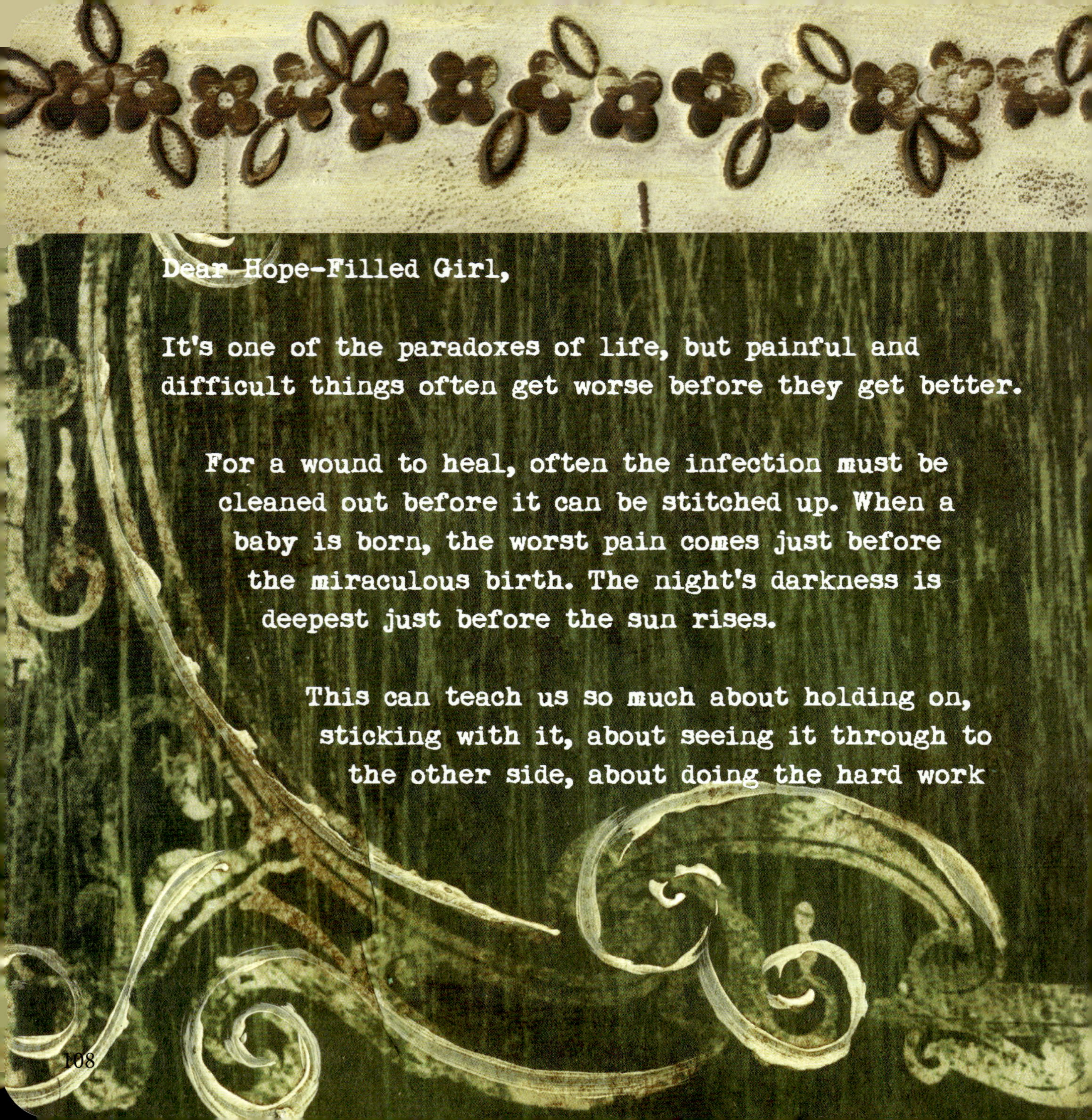

Dear Hope-Filled Girl,

It's one of the paradoxes of life, but painful and difficult things often get worse before they get better.

For a wound to heal, often the infection must be cleaned out before it can be stitched up. When a baby is born, the worst pain comes just before the miraculous birth. The night's darkness is deepest just before the sun rises.

This can teach us so much about holding on, sticking with it, about seeing it through to the other side, about doing the hard work

of digging out the infection
no matter how painful it is...
so that we can fully HEAL.

There is nothing like holding a
new baby after the pain of childbirth.
There is no more beautiful sight than
the sunrise after a long dark night.

Would we be able to feel the incredible miracles, the
beauty, the joy, the peace...if we didn't know the pain?

Stick with it, beautiful girl. You'll be glad
that you did. You are so so soooooo loved.
xoxo

make life
beautiful

Dear Unforgettable Girl,

Think about your favorite song, your favorite work of art, your favorite piece of clothing. Think about the chair you are sitting on and the room you are in.

Someone, somewhere, at some time, had a crazy idea. It was scary to tell others about it. It was scary to make that idea materialize and then to put it out into the world for others to see, use, enjoy...and judge.

What if the person who wrote your favorite song stayed too afraid to share it? What if your favorite work of art stayed under the artist's bed and was never seen by another pair of eyes aside from her own?

YOU have a message. YOU have a mission. YOU have a purpose...one that is unique to you and will never be duplicated by another human being, ever.
In the beautiful words of Charles D. Gill: "There are many wonderful things that will never be done if YOU do not do them."
The world needs you and your beautiful heart. Be brave...share those parts of yourself. YOU CAN DO IT!
You are loved. xoxo

Be a light

in the darkness

Dear Radiant Girl,

Every day our skin gets a little older and things start to fall that used to be so firm. Wrinkles show up and our hair changes. Little soft pooches show up here and there.

Everything changes. This is the beautiful, intended process of life, yet we beat ourselves up when it begins to happen to us.

Your beauty is in those eyes of yours, where stories of years and years of living have made them sparkle with beautiful wisdom. Your incredible stop-traffic gorgeousness is in those hands of yours, hands that create so many things and help and nuture so many people. YOUR RADIANT BEAUTY shines out from that beautiful, pure, kind and good heart of yours...the heart that lights up the world and shines a warm glow on EVERY face to make it more beautiful.

Plaase don't steal away the beauty of this time in your life by wishing you still looked like a kid, phenomenal you.

We all get to take turns being kids, being teenagers, being young adults...and then we get to take turns at every stage of wise and wonderful womanhood.

When we embrace the beauty of every stage of life, we can be the most beautiful creatures that ever walked the earth.

This is what you were created to be.

Who you are today is exactly right. Bless your hands and your eyes and your mind and your heart.

You are so loved.
xoxo

you are a
beautiful soul

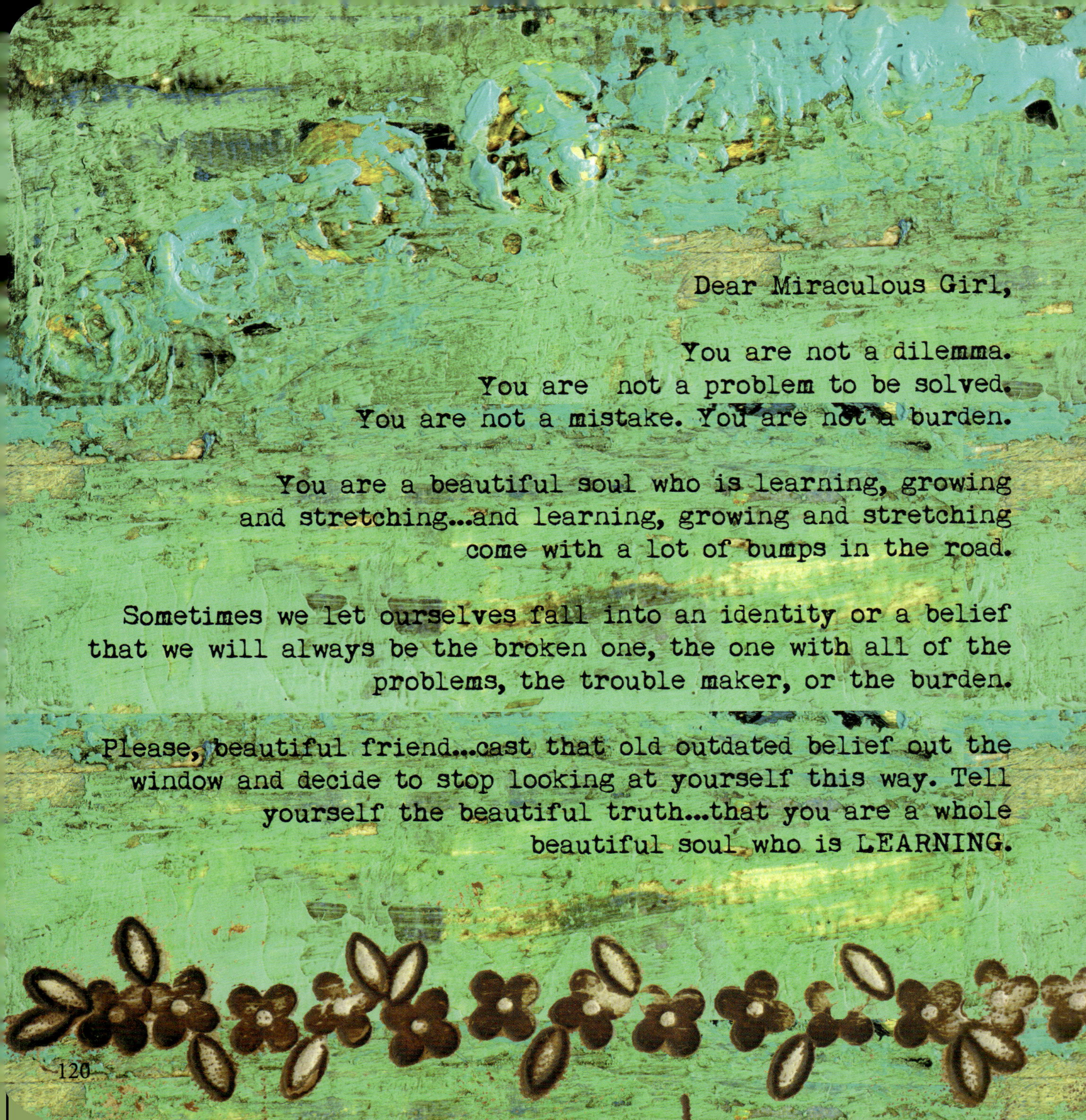

Dear Miraculous Girl,

You are not a dilemma.
You are not a problem to be solved.
You are not a mistake. You are not a burden.

You are a beautiful soul who is learning, growing and stretching...and learning, growing and stretching come with a lot of bumps in the road.

Sometimes we let ourselves fall into an identity or a belief that we will always be the broken one, the one with all of the problems, the trouble maker, or the burden.

Please, beautiful friend...cast that old outdated belief out the window and decide to stop looking at yourself this way. Tell yourself the beautiful truth...that you are a whole beautiful soul who is LEARNING.

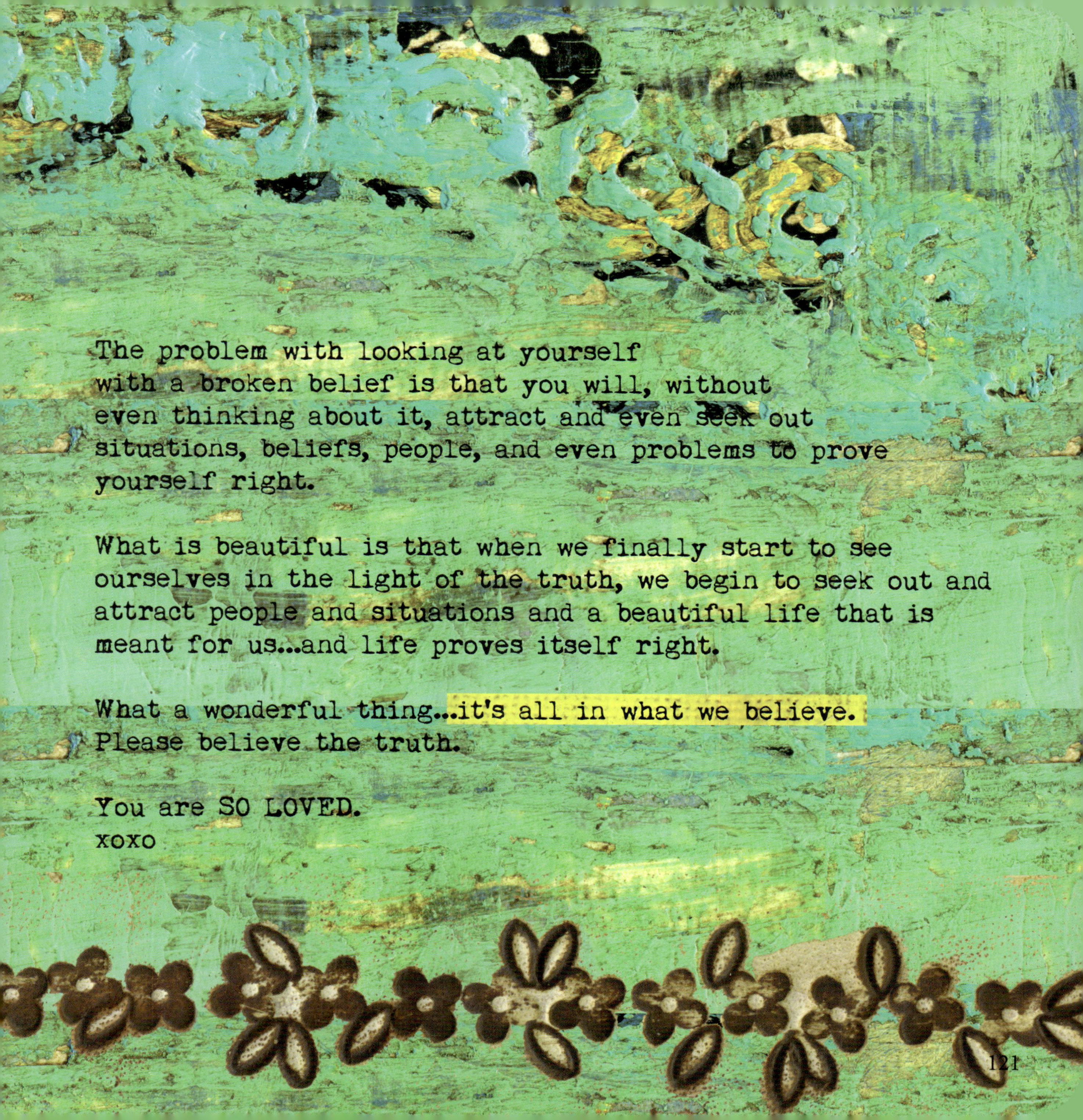

The problem with looking at yourself
with a broken belief is that you will, without
even thinking about it, attract and even seek out
situations, beliefs, people, and even problems to prove
yourself right.

What is beautiful is that when we finally start to see
ourselves in the light of the truth, we begin to seek out and
attract people and situations and a beautiful life that is
meant for us...and life proves itself right.

What a wonderful thing...it's all in what we believe.
Please believe the truth.

You are SO LOVED.
xoxo

beautiful
TRUTH

Dear Beautiful Soulful Girl,

I wonder if you know how loved you are.

I wonder if you know how valuable and unique and wonderful you are.

I wonder if you realize that the colors in the sunset and the way light ripples off the water and the perfect little delicate flower petals...

...all were made just for YOU to enjoy and to remind you every day of the miracle of your own life.

I wonder if you see the perfectly imperfect way your life has unfolded up to this point, and how everything you have lived through has made you into the phenomenal woman you are today.

I wonder if you realize that difficult things do not always happen TO you, but they happen FOR you.

I wonder if you know.

And if you didn't..I hope you know now.

You are so very very loved.
xoxo

about

ABOUT THE AUTHOR

Melody Ross has been a worldwide known artist and entrepreneur since her twenties, building one of the most collected and sought after brands in the designer paper industry and designing hundreds of products for many other companies.

It was a serious life trauma, however, that put her on the path of her life's work. In 2004 her beloved high school sweetheart and husband of 14 years sustained a brain injury that turned their life upside down. Over the 6 years of his recovery, they lost seemingly everything that they had spent the first part of their life building together, but painstakingly kept their marriage and family together. Through this experience, Melody learned countless lessons that she vowed to share if their life were to turn around. After many difficult years, her husband made a complete recovery.

In 2009, Melody walked away from her first company and started Brave Girls Club with her sister, Kathy....and every day has been a beautiful wild adventure of doing everything she loves most with all of the people she loves most.

Melody and Marq have 5 chidren and live on a beautiful ranch in Idaho where Melody makes art in the turquoise barn, grows every flower imaginable and hosts brave girls from all over the world....teaching them everything she knows about the healing power of unconditional love.

to learn more about melody
www.melodyross.com

ABOUT BRAVE GIRLS CLUB

It all started as a big idea...many years before it became a reality...but once it did..it grew quickly and beautifully and all over the world. Brave Girls Club continues to grow day by day.

Sisters Melody and Kathy talked about what their dream job would be and decided that creating a beautiful, safe, creative, loving & fun place for women to heal, grow and move forward was a perfect match for the skills that they each had, skills that perfectly complimented each other. In 2009. they both walked away from their careers, and jumped with both feet into BGC to never look back.

BGC now hosts world class art retreats, life changing online courses and has one of the most beautiful online stores & online communities to be found.

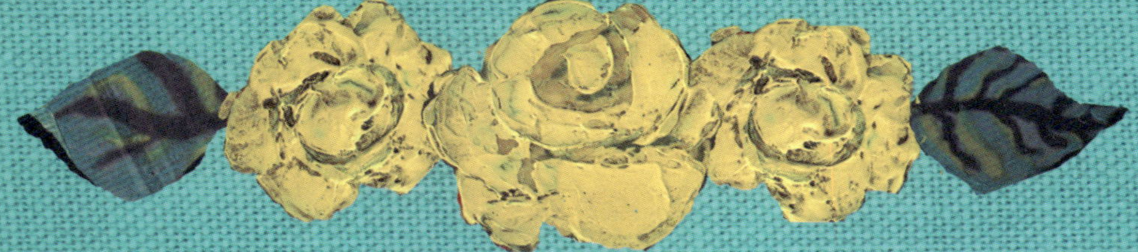

Brave Girls Club is for every girl and every woman who wants to be brave enough to go and live the big beautiful life that is just right for them...because that means something different for each of us. To learn more and to sign up for our daily happy email, called "A Little Bird Told Me"

go to
www.bravegirlsclub.com
(be sure to check out the online shoppe.... full of pretty things!)

it really was written
just for YOU.